De.

MW00528690

& a great Christian example

Keep up the Good Work

Love, Hilda

Mini-Moments
for
Leaders

Mini-Moments for Leaders

by Robert Strand

New Leaf Press

First printing: July 1996

ISBN: 0-89221-331-0
Library of Congress Catalog No. 96-69686

Presented to:

_____

Presented by:

_____

Date:

_____

What Is Leadership?

Lots of people talk about it but few really understand it! Most people want it but very few really achieve it! What is this thing called leadership?

In the simplest of terms: LEADERSHIP IS INFLUENCE! That's all . . . nothing more and nothing less. Leadership is influence . . . influence is leadership.

James C. Georges said: "What is leadership? Remove for a moment the moral issues behind it, and there is only one definition: *LEADERSHIP IS THE ABILITY TO OBTAIN FOLLOWERS.* Hitler was a leader and so was Jim Jones. Jesus of Nazareth, Martin Luther King Jr., Winston Churchill, and John F. Kennedy all were leaders. While their value systems and management abilities were very different, each had followers.

"Once you define leadership as the ability to get followers, you work backward from that point of reference to figure out how to lead."[1]

He who thinketh he leadeth and hath no one
following him is only taking a walk!

*As Jesus went on from there, He saw a
man named Matthew sitting at the tax
collector's booth. "Follow me," He
told him, and Matthew got up and
followed Him* (Matt. 9:9).

Little Known Olympian

Quick . . . who would you say was the world's greatest all-around female athlete in history? If you said, Fanny Blankers-Koen of the Netherlands, you are right!

Following the 1936 Olympics, she emerged as the world's greatest female sprinter, but the 1940 and 1944 games were canceled due to World War II. She married, gave birth to a son and daughter, and again at age 30 competed in the 1948 Olympics in London.

Fanny won the 100 meter dash, 80 meter hurdles, 200 meter dash, and the 4 x 100 relay! She is the only woman to have won four track and field gold medals in the same Olympiad. Fanny was also the world's record holder in the long jump and the high jump, but elected not to compete in these additional events.

When interviewed and asked her secret to winning, she replied: "Continual training and perseverance!"

Excellence is to do a common thing in an
uncommon way. (Booker T. Washington)

*I do not consider myself yet to have
taken hold of it. But one thing I do:
Forgetting what is behind and
straining toward what is ahead, I press
on toward the goal to win the prize for
which God has called me*
(Phil. 3:13-14).

Lighten Up

"The only advice some of my clients need can be summed up in two words: LIGHTEN UP! It's ironic, but your career can depend on whether you're willing to get serious about taking yourself less seriously," so writes Roger Ailes, chairman of Ailes Communications.

According to executive recruiters, for seven out of ten people who lose their jobs, the cause isn't a lack of skill . . . it's personality conflicts.

The management newsletter *Bottom Line Personal* reports, "As an executive reaches middle management and beyond, the primary criteria for advancement are communication and motivation skills, rather than job performance. Relations with superiors and peers are critical."

The bottom line is simply this: Top management promotes the people it likes!

Be more concerned with your character than
with your reputation. Your character is what
you really are, while your reputation is merely
what others think you are. (John Wooden)

*A cheerful heart is good medicine, but
a crushed spirit dries up the bones*
(Prov. 17:22).

He who has confidence in

himself will lead the rest.

Horace Bushnell (1802 - 1876)

Table Manners

Ever been invited to the White House for dinner? Few of us have. It's an occasion certainly for one to mind one's P's and Q's. This same thought was on the minds of several Vermont friends, who were leaders in their fields, as they dined with President Calvin Coolidge. The dinner passed uneventfully until coffee was served. The president poured his into a saucer. Eager to please, these guests did the same. Then Coolidge added cream and sugar. The visitors did likewise. Then Coolidge leaned over and gave his saucer of coffee to the cat!

I love it! I just wish I could have been there to watch it. Peer pressure is awesome! Good friends can be good for us . . . bad friends can be very bad for us. Leaders are people who are careful of the friends they make. Leaders are looking for people who can challenge them, lift their sights, pull up their expectations, mentor them, be an example. Leaders are not blind followers.

My best friend is the one who brings out the
best in me. (Henry Ford)

Two are better than one, because they
have a good return for their work: If
one falls down, his friend can help him
up. But pity the man who falls and has
no one to help him up!
(Eccles. 4:9-10).

Finish the Race

At 7:00 p.m., October 20, 1968, just a few thousand spectators remained in the Mexico City Olympic Stadium. More than an hour earlier, Mamo Wolde of Ethiopia had won this marathon. The spectators were startled by sirens and looked toward the marathon gate . . . a lone figure, John Stephen Akhwari of Tanzania, appeared as the last runner in the race.

One leg was bloodied and bandaged . . . he grimaced with each step. He'd injured it in a fall. He painfully hobbled around the track and crossed the finish line with the crowd cheering.

A reporter wrote: "Today we have seen a young African runner who symbolizes the finest in the human spirit. . . ."

Akhwari was asked why he hadn't quit. He replied, "My country did not send me . . . to start, they sent me 7,000 miles to FINISH the race!"

Leaders are people who finish their assignments!

The difference between a successful person
and others is not a lack of strength, not a lack
of knowledge, but rather in a lack of will.
(Vince Lombardi)

I have fought the good fight, I have
finished the race, I have kept the faith
(1 Tim. 4:7).

Priorities

Perhaps you remember it . . . I'm talking about the Eastern Airlines jumbo jet that crashed in the Florida Everglades. The plane was the now-infamous Flight 401, bound from New York to Miami with a heavy load of holiday passengers. As the plane approached the Miami airport for its landing, the light that indicates proper deployment of the landing gear failed to light. The plane then flew in a large, looping circle over the swamps of the Everglades while the cockpit crew checked to see if the gear had deployed or if the bulb was defective.

When the flight engineer attempted to remove the light bulb, it wouldn't budge and the other members of the crew tried to help. As they struggled with the bulb, no one noticed that the aircraft was losing altitude until the plane just flew right into the swamp!

Dozens of people lost their lives while an experienced crew of high-priced pilots fiddled with a 75-cent light bulb. Too often, little things can trip up leaders. Keep your priorities straight!

> The price of greatness is responsibility.
> (Winston Churchill)

> *And now, what does the Lord your God*
> *ask of you but to fear the Lord your*
> *God, to walk in all His ways, to love*
> *Him, to serve the Lord your God with*
> *all your heart and with all your soul,*
> *and to observe the Lord's commands*
> *and decrees that I am giving you today*
> *for your own good?* (Deut. 10:12-13).

My Influence

My life shall touch a dozen lives
    Before this day is done.
        Leave countless marks of good or ill,
            E'er sets the evening sun.

This, the wish I always wish,
    The prayer I always pray:
        Lord, may my life help other lives
            It touches by the way.[2]

Everyone is a leader because everyone
influences someone. Not everyone will
become a great leader, but everyone can
become a better leader. (John Maxwell)

Let your light shine before men, that
they may see your good deeds and
praise your Father in heaven
(Matt. 5:16).

Ockham's Razor

One of the earlier practitioners of work simplification was William of Ockham. This man lived in England about 600 years ago. He was a graduate of Oxford University.

William's trouble came to a head when he tangled with ecclesiastical authorities on a moot problem of the day. He contended that the church should confine itself to the business of saving souls, not messing around with government or business. He raised such a fuss that the powers that be decided to get rid of him. He escaped to another country and there went to work sharpening up the tool which later became known as "Ockham's Razor."

What is it? This "Razor of Ockham" is simply a method of thinking which cuts directly to the core of any problem, separating the essentials from the non-essentials, removing all unnecessary facts of the problem. Nothing is left but the bare bones of the problem.

This "tool" has become an important element in every leader's management kit.

THE LEADER'S PRAYER:
Lord, when I am wrong, make me willing to change; when I am right, make me easy to live with. So strengthen me that the power of example will far exceed the authority of my rank. (Pauline H. Peters)

I urge you to live a life worthy of the calling you have received. Be completely humble and gentle; be patient, bearing with one another in love (Eph. 4:1-2).

The lure of power can separate the most resolute of Christians from the true nature of Christian leadership, which is service to others. It's difficult to stand on a pedestal and wash the feet of those below.

Charles Colson

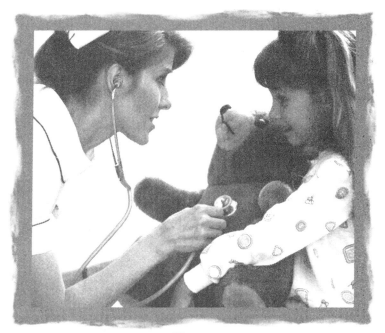

Let There Be No Extremes in Leadership

Self-reliant but not self-sufficient,
Conscientious but not a perfectionist,
Energetic but not self-seeking,
Disciplined but not demanding,
Steadfast but not stubborn,
Generous but not gullible,
Tactful but not timid,
Meek but not weak,
Serious but not sullen,
Humorous but not hilarious,
Loyal but not sectarian,
Friendly but not familiar,
Unmovable but not stationary,
Holy but not holier-than-thou,

Gentle but not hypersensitive,
　　Discerning but not critical,
Tenderhearted but not touchy,
　　Progressive but not pretentious.

We too often love things and use people . . .
when we should be using things and loving
people.

*You . . . were called to be free. But do not use your
freedom to indulge the sinful nature; rather, serve
one another in love. The entire law is summed up
in a single command: "Love your neighbor as
yourself"* (Gal. 5:13-14).

Leader or Boss?

H. Gordon Selfridge built one of the world's largest department stores in London. He states that he achieved success by being a leader, not a boss. Here is his own comparison of the two types of executives and their two different styles:

The boss drives his people . . . the LEADER coaches them.
The boss depends on authority . . . the LEADER on good will.
The boss inspires fear . . . the LEADER inspires enthusiasm.
The boss says "I" . . . the LEADER says "we."
The boss fixes the blame for the breakdown . . . the LEADER
    fixes the breakdown.
The boss knows how it is done . . . the LEADER shows how it is
    done.
The boss says "Go" . . . the LEADER says "Let's go!"

The Sunshine Magazine

Leadership is the art of getting someone else to do something that you want done because he wants to do it. (Dwight D. Eisenhower)

Be strong and courageous, because you will lead these people to inherit the land I swore to their forefathers to give them. Be strong and very courageous. Be careful to obey all the law . . . do not turn from it to the right or to the left, that you may be successful wherever you go (Josh. 1:6-7).

Choose to Die or Choose to Change

During the 1920s through the 1940s the Swiss watch was the most prestigious and best quality watch you could buy in the world! As a result, about 80 percent of the watches sold in the world were made in Switzerland. It was a proud industry with a wonderful product.

In the late 1950s the digital watch was presented to some of the leaders of the Swiss watch companies. They rejected the idea because they knew they already had the best watches and the best watchmakers. The man who had invented and developed the digital watch finally sold the concept to Seiko of Japan. In the 1940s, Swiss watch-making companies employed some eighty thousand people. Today, they employ less than eighteen thousand! In the 1940s, 80 percent of the watches sold were Swiss made. Today 80 percent of the watches are digital.

This true story represents what happens too frequently to people and organizations: We choose to die rather than choose to change!

If at first you don't succeed, failure may be your thing. (Larry Anderson)

And no one pours new wine into old wineskins. If he does, the wine will burst the skins, and both the wine and the wineskins will be ruined. No, he pours new wine into new wineskins (Mark 2:22).

Can't Spel . . . Just Sel

Did you hear about the newly hired salesperson who faxed his first sales report back to the home office? It stunned the brass in the sales department because of the atrocious spelling. This is what he wrote: "I seen this hear outfit which ain't never bot a dim's worth of nowthin from us and I sole them about a qartr millyon. I'm on my way to Chicawgo."

Before the man could be given the heave-ho by the sales manager who was concerned about image, came this fax from Chicago: "I cum hear and sole them haff a millyon."

Fearful if he did, and afraid if he didn't fire the ignorant, poor spelling salesman, the sales manager dumped the problem in the lap of the president. The next morning, the ivory-towered sales department members were stunned to see posted above the two faxes this memo from the president: "We ben spendin two much time trying to spel instead of trying to sel. Let's watch those sails. I want everbody should read these faxes from Gooch who is on the rode doin a grate job for us and you should go and do like he done."

A leader becomes a great leader because of
his or her ability to empower others.

> *He told them, "The harvest is plentiful,*
> *but the workers are few. Ask the Lord*
> *of the harvest, therefore, to send out*
> *workers into His harvest field. Go! I*
> *am sending you out like lambs among*
> *wolves" (Luke 10:2-3).*

Henry Ford and Change

Robert Lacy has written a book, *Ford: the Man and the Machine*. In it, Lacy says Ford was a man who loved his Model T so much he didn't want to change even a bolt on it. He kicked out William Knudsen, because Knudsen thought he saw the sun setting on the Model T in 1912. Ford went to a Highland Park garage and saw the new design created by Knudsen.

On-the-scene mechanics tell the story of how Ford went berserk. He spied the gleaming red lacquer paint on a new, low-slung version of the Model T. One eyewitness said, "Ford had his hands in his pockets, and he walked around that car three or four times. It was a four-door job, and the top was down. Finally, he got to the left-hand side of the car, and he takes his hands out, gets hold of the door, and bang! He ripped the door right off! How the man did it, I don't know! He jumped in there, and bang goes the other door. Bang goes the windshield. He jumps over the back seat and starts pounding on the top. He rips the top with the heel of his shoe. He wrecked the car as much as he could." He wanted life to stop where it was!

The more you change, the more you become
an instrument of change in the lives of others.
If you want to become a change agent, you
also must change. (Howard Hendricks)

*Therefore, if anyone is in Christ, he is
a new creation; the old has gone, the
new has come!* (2 Cor. 5:17).

*Leaders are ordinary people
with extraordinary
determination.*

A First Lady Speaks

This was excerpted from a radio speech by Madame Chiang Kai-shek, first lady and the inspirational bulwark of the Chinese people in their struggles during World War II:

If the past has taught us anything, it is that every cause brings its effect, every action has a consequence. We Chinese have a saying: "If a man plants melons he will reap melons; if he sows beans, he will reap beans." And this is true of everyone's life; good begets good, and evil leads to evil.

In the end, we are all the sum total of our actions. Character cannot be counterfeited, nor can it be put on and cast off as if it were a garment to meet the whim of the moment. Like the markings on wood which are ingrained in the very heart of the tree, character requires time and nurturing for growth and development. Thus also, day by day, we write our own destiny; for inexorably . . . we become what we do."

Character cannot be counterfeited, nor can it
be put on and cast off.
(Madame Chiang Kai-shek)

*Better a poor man whose walk is
blameless than a rich man whose ways
are perverse* (Prov. 28:6).

What Are You Passing On?

Think about it . . . isn't it amazing how we pass on our own hang-ups to others. We do this to our kids, our employees, and people we influence.

Reminds me of the old story about the newly married bride who cooked a ham dinner for her husband. Before she put in the pan, she cut off both ends of the ham. When her husband asked her why she did that, she replied that her mother had always cooked hams that way.

Later, when they were having a baked ham dinner at her mother's home, he asked her, casually, why she cut both ends off the ham. The mother shrugged and said she didn't really know, except that her mother had always done it that way.

Finally, he asked the grandmother why she always cut the ends off the ham before she baked it. She looked at him, suspiciously, replying, "Because my baking dish is too small!"

Every job is a self-portrait of the person who
did it. Autograph your work with excellence.

Cast your bread upon the waters, for
after many days you will find it again
(Eccles. 11:1).

The Second Chance

When you hear the name Alfred Nobel, you naturally think of the "Nobel Peace Prize." But that's really chapter two of this man's story. Alfred Nobel was the Swedish chemist who made a huge fortune by inventing dynamite and other powerful explosives used for weapons of war. When his brother died, one newspaper accidentally printed the obituary for Alfred instead. It described the dead man as one who had become rich by enabling people to kill each other in unprecedented numbers.

Shaken by this assessment of his life, Alfred Nobel resolved to use his fortune from then on to award accomplishments that benefited humanity. He became a philanthropist and created the coveted NOBEL PEACE PRIZE which is awarded to special accomplishments in a variety of fields annually. What a rare opportunity . . . Nobel was able to read his obituary and life evaluation but had the possibility of living long enough to change that assessment of his life.

In the end, it is important to remember that we cannot become what we need to be by remaining what we are. (Max Depree)

This is how we know who the children of God are and who the children of the devil are: Anyone who does not do what is right is not a child of God; nor is anyone who does not love his brother (1 John 3:10).

Volunteering and Your Good Health

Recent medical research indicates that helping your cause to raise gifts by giving volunteer time may be one of the more healthy things you can do! Epidemiologist James House, University of Michigan, studied 2,700 people for over a decade. More than *any other activity, he found that doing regular volunteer work increased the average person's life expectancy and vitality!*

For example . . . men who did no volunteer work were 2-1/2 times more likely to have died during the study than men who volunteered once a week! Why? It's a way of connecting with people and that's healthy! It reduces stress and seems good for your immune system, too.

Leaders are people who are interested in others as people. Leaders help others to be compassionate. Besides, it improves physical health and spiritual well being!

Those who love deeply never grow old; they
may die of old age, but they die young.
(Ladies Home Journal)

*And if anyone gives even a cup of cold
water to one of these little ones
because he is my disciple, I tell you the
truth, he will certainly not lose his
reward* (Matt. 10:42).

I believe it might be accepted as a
fairly reliable rule of thumb that
the man who is ambitious to lead
is disqualified as a leader.

A.W. Tozer (1897 - 1963)

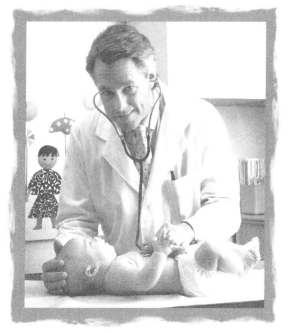

Something to Shoot For

Olympic gold medal heptathlon champion Jackie Joyner-Kersee was born in impoverished East St. Louis. From her mother, she learned a host of values . . . modesty, faith, hard work, love, and perseverance.

"My mother was only a child herself, raising a child," Joyner-Kersee says. "She wanted to protect me. I couldn't wear flashy clothes, and I wasn't allowed to date until I was 18. We were so poor that I never asked for anything; instead I immersed myself in school and sports."

The pride her mother instilled paid off for Jackie. She graduated in the top 10 percent of her class and set a state high school long-jump record. "I never despaired," she says, "I always had something to shoot for. I kept telling myself, you've got to work hard; you've got to be successful."

There aren't any hard and fast rules for
succeeding in the world . . . just hard ones.

*Make it your ambition to lead a quiet
life, to mind your business and to work
with your hands, just as we told you,
so that your daily life may win the
respect of outsiders and so that you
will not be dependent on anybody*
(1 Thess. 4:11-12).

Make Them Proud

In his first 12 seasons as manager of the Los Angeles Dodgers, Tommy Lasorda led his team to six division titles, four pennants, and two World Series victories. After the 1988 series, columnist Jonathan Rand noted: "Tommy Lasorda does not have an off switch."

Lasorda credits the inspiration for his managing style to a can of evaporated milk he spotted on his kitchen table when he was 15. It read, "Contented cows give better milk."

As Lasorda himself puts it: "I am of the belief that contented people give better performances. I try to make it fun for them. I try to make them proud of the organization they represent!"

One of the tasks of a leader is to build better people, to encourage people to become better people, to challenge people to make the best of their talents, and to inspire them to reach for higher goals. Thanks to Tommy Lasorda for one more life lesson on leadership.

Wisdom is knowing what to do next, skill is
knowing how to do it, and virtue is doing it.
(Everywoman's Family Circle)

> *But godliness with contentment is*
> *great gain. For we brought nothing*
> *into the world, and we can take*
> *nothing out of it. But if we have food*
> *and clothing, we will be content with*
> *that* (1 Tim. 6:6-8).

Leader or Loser . . . Part I

A LEADER believes in taking positive actions . . .
A loser believes in blind fate.
A LEADER works through the problems . . .
A loser stands around and talks and talks about it.
A LEADER knows what the real issues are, what to fight for . . .
A loser compromises.
A LEADER is not afraid of losing . . .
A loser is not going to take a chance.
A LEADER looks for the good in any and every situation . . .
A loser looks for what is wrong and somebody to blame.
A LEADER is always growing and learning . . .
A loser considers himself an expert and already knows everything.

It takes a person with character to get up and
try again if he or she falls.

*A man's wisdom gives him patience; it
is to his glory to overlook an offense*
(Prov. 19:11).

Leader or Loser . . . Part II

A LEADER is considerate and cares for others . . .

A loser cares only for himself/herself.

A LEADER is a good listener . . .

A loser waits for his time to talk.

A LEADER does things a loser wouldn't think of doing
and plans ahead . . .

A loser is always too busy to do the hard things.

A LEADER has a healthy sense of humor . . .

A loser is a whiner and blamer.

A LEADER is not afraid to make long or
short range commitments . . .

A loser makes promises.

A LEADER never quits . . .

A loser never wins.

Your attitude in living will determine your
attitude in leading.

*Enlarge the place of your tent, stretch
your tent curtains wide, do not hold
back; lengthen your cords, strengthen
your stakes* (Isa. 54:2).

Poor Decisions

Roger Freed is a former major league baseball player who served with five different teams during the 1970s, a journeyman player with a lifetime batting average of .245. He became a symbol of how poor management can result in failure. During the '77 season, the Cardinals were playing the Phillies in Veteran Stadium. With pinch-hitting help from Freed, St. Louis tied the score in the top of the ninth. However, when the Phillies came to bat, Freed was placed in right field by Cardinals manager Vern Rapp.

Cardinals broadcaster Jack Buck was incredulous and concerned that Freed, a career back-up first baseman, had been left in the game on defense. Buck was prophetic. With two outs and the winning run on base for the Phillies, the batter hit a fly ball to Freed. "Freed drops the ball!" exclaimed a stunned Buck. "The Phillies have won the game! Unbelievable!"

Rapp was fired. Poor decisions like the one he made in Philadelphia cost Rapp his job.

Selecting the right people is 75 percent of organizational success. (Edward R. Dayton)

Choose seven men from among you who are known to be full of the Spirit and wisdom. We will turn this responsibility over to them (Acts 6:3).

If we work upon marble, it will perish. If we work upon brass, time will efface it. If we rear temples, they will crumble to dust. But if we work upon men's immortal minds, if we imbue them with high principles, with the just fear of God and love of their fellowmen, we engrave on those tablets something which no time can efface and which will brighten to all eternity.

Daniel Webster (1892 - 1952)

Leaders Take Responsibility

Bo Schembechler, former football coach of the University of Michigan, relates this story about the third game of their 1970 season: His Wolverines were playing Texas A&M and couldn't seem to move the ball against their defense. Everything they tried seemed to be stopped. Then, quickly, between plays, Dan Dierdorf, one of their offensive lineman . . . who was probably the best college lineman in the country at that time . . . came running over to the sidelines. Fed up and unhappy with the team's performance on offense, he yelled at Schembechler and anybody else who could hear him on the sidelines. "Listen, coach! Run every play over me! Over me! Every play!" They did. Michigan then ran off-tackle six times in a row and marched down the field. Michigan won that game!

When the game is on the line, leaders take responsibility for leading their teams on to victory!

Leaders never place themselves above their followers . . . except in carrying our responsibilities.

Next to him was Eleazar son of Dodai the Ahohite. As one of the three mighty men, he was with David when they taunted the Philistines gathered at Pas Dammim for battle. Then the men of Israel retreated, but he stood his ground and struck down the Philistines till his hand grew tired and froze to the sword. The Lord brought a great victory that day (2 Sam. 23:9-10).

Just One Little Problem

The sales manager of a dog food company asked his salespeople how they liked the company's new advertising program. "Great! Best in the business!" the salespeople said.

"How do you like our new label and package?"

"Great! Best in the business!" the salespeople responded.

"How do you like our sales force?"

They were the sales force and they had to admit they were good. "Okay, then," said the manager. "So we've got the best label, the best package, and the best advertising program being sold by the best sales force in the business. Tell me why we are in 15th place in the dog food business?"

There was silence . . . finally, after a long wait, one salesman from the back of the room said, "It's those lousy dogs. They won't eat the stuff!"

The unexamined life is not worth living.
(Plato)

By their fruit you will recognize them.
Do people pick grapes from
thornbushes, or figs from thistles?
Likewise every good tree bears good
fruit, but a bad tree bears bad fruit . . .
thus, by their fruit you will recognize
them (Matt. 7:16-17, 20).

Oh, Well

Mack Sennett, in the *Book of Blunders*, writes the following: It happened to be a wet day in sunny Southern California, and the street in front of the Keystone was about half an inch deep in mud and water. Chester Conklin spied Mable Normand across the street, standing on the curb, wondering how to get across, and so he made a fancy gesture. He bowed like a headwaiter expecting a $50 tip, snatched off his coat, and spread it in the mud for Mable to step on. She stepped . . . and disappeared into an open manhole![3]

Ever have a day like that? Sure, most of us have, and if you haven't, you will! Sometimes, the very best of intentions don't seem to come out all right or as planned. Life has a way. So what do we do when the unthinkable happens? Apologize, make it right, do restitution, admit your mistake, ask forgiveness, pray that you don't do it again, and go on!

The most important single ingredient to the
formula of success is knowing how to get
along with people. (Teddy Roosevelt)

*You . . . were called to be free. But do
not use your freedom to indulge the
sinful nature; rather, serve one another
in love. The entire law is summed up in
a single command: "Love your
neighbor as yourself"* (Gal. 5:13-14).

Early Influence

"Values are the emotional rules by which a society organizes and disciplines itself," notes master storyteller James A. Michener. "Without them, nations . . . and individuals . . . can run amok."

"In my teens," Michener recalls, "I was a vagabond riding the rails. But earlier I had learned some ironclad values in the home of my adoptive mother. This fine, hard-working woman always read to us at night. By the time I was five, I had the great rhythm of the English language echoing in my mind. I learned values in church and in school, where a high school athletic coach took me . . . fatherless and without a rudder . . . and steered me in the right direction."

Values are more caught than taught. One of the responsibilities of a leader is to be a mentor, a coach, a teacher, to help somebody else along life's way. Leadership is developing your most important asset: PEOPLE!

Trust men and they will be true to you; treat
them greatly and they will show themselves
great. (Ralph Waldo Emerson)

*Each of you should look not only to
your own interests, but also to the
interests of others* (Phil. 2:4).

While yielding to loving parental leadership, children are also learning to yield to the benevolent leadership of God himself.

James C. Dobson

Important People

When Harry S. Truman returned home to Independence, Missouri, for the purpose of casting his vote in the 1948 elections, a group of media people were assigned to stay close to him at all times. They landed at the Kansas City airport and discovered that the president had already arrived and was motoring on his way home.

Quickly they assembled a noisy police escort which scattered traffic out of their way as they raced after him in their press cars. But when they reached his home, Truman was not there. Not knowing what to do, they just waited for his arrival some time later. When he arrived, one of those worried reporters asked him what had happened to detain him.

"Oh," said Truman, "we were stopped by the police and had to pull over and wait. Seems there were some very important people going through town!"

How refreshing . . . modest, even. A rare commodity in today's world.

> The people who have a right to boast usually
> don't need to.

*Like clouds and wind without rain is a
man who boasts of gifts he does not
give* (Prov. 25:14).

Visit the Cemetery

A business man, harassed, stressed, haggard, burned out, and discouraged from overwork, took his many problems to his psychiatrist. After a short examination, the doctor promptly prescribed less work. "Furthermore," said the doctor, "I want you to spend one hour each week in the cemetery."

"What on earth do you want me to do that for? I'm too busy to do that. Besides, what should I do in the cemetery?"

The doctor patiently replied, "Not much. Take it easy, saunter around, and look at the gravemarkers. Get acquainted with some of the people already in there and remember that one of these days, you'll be there, too. Also, remember, they didn't finish their work, either. Nobody does, you know."

I'm for living with a correct perspective on life and work and the hereafter.

It's not the load of life and business that breaks you down . . . it's the way you carry it.

Come to Me, all you who are weary and burdened, and I will give you rest. Take My yoke upon you and learn from Me, for I am gentle and humble in heart, and you will find rest for your souls. For My yoke is easy and My burden is light (Matt. 11:28-30).

Too Soon to Quit

There was this young boy attempting to learn how to ice skate. He had fallen so many times that his face was cut and the blood and tears ran together. But he'd get up another time and try it again . . . and fall, get up, again. . . .

Someone, finally, out of sympathy, skated over to the little guy, picked him up and kindly said, "Son, why don't you quit? You're just going to kill yourself if you don't."

The boy brushed the tears from his eyes and said, "Mister, I didn't buy these skates to learn how to quit! I bought them to learn how to skate!"

You've heard it said: IT'S ALWAYS TOO SOON TO QUIT! Hang in there, persevere! Who knows, perhaps tomorrow you'll experience your breakthrough! Your answer may be just around the corner! It's the people who persevere to the end who make it!

Perseverance is defined as sticking with
something you're not really stuck on.

*Blessed is the man who perseveres
under trial, because when he has stood
the test, he will receive the crown of
life that God has promised to those
who love Him* (James 1:12).

Life Is Wonderful

A patient in the doctor's waiting room heard a scream from within the doctor's examining room. Then, an elderly lady burst out of the door and quickly departed, obviously agitated.

"What happened?" asked the waiting patient.

"I told her she was pregnant," replied the doctor.

"You couldn't be serious," remarked the patient.

"Of course not," the doctor answered, "but it cured her hiccups!"

THEN . . . there was the man taking his grandfather clock to be repaired, rounded a corner and ran right into another man, sending him sprawling. After receiving profuse apologies, the man on the ground got up, dusted himself off, and snarled, "Why don't you wear a watch like everybody else?"

So what's the principle? All of us need to laugh, especially leaders, because it's good therapy.

Imagination was given to us to compensate
for what we are not and a sense of humor to
console us for what we are.

A cheerful heart is good medicine, but
a crushed spirit dries up the bones
(Prov. 17:22).

Doing Business in Egypt

If you are in business and you'd like to expand into the Egyptian market, the magazine *Nation's Business* (6/87) had this advice:

Friendship is the first step toward successful business in Egypt. Canny American traders invite a business prospect out for a meal before even thinking of broaching a serious commercial subject. To "eat bread and salt" with a man . . . an Egyptian expression . . . is to bind the friendship to obligate one man to another. Taking nourishment with an Egyptian is serious business. The table is a friendly place.

Americans are advised not to treat the meal casually. Invite your prospect to the best restaurant and be a generous host!

Now . . . isn't that a pretty good piece of advice for building all relationships? Leadership is influence which is built on relationship.

Relationship is a living thing that lasts only so
long as it is nourished with kindness,
sympathy, loyalty, integrity, and
understanding.

*He who covers over an offense
promotes love, but whoever repeats the
matter separates close friends*
(Prov. 17:9).

One of the marks of true greatness is the ability to develop greatness in others.

J.C. Macaulay

Forgetting the Past Mistakes

In his autobiography, *The Tumult and the Shouting*, the great sports columnist Grantland Rice gives this advice about mistakes:

"Because golf exposes the flaws of the human swing . . . a basically simple maneuver . . . it causes more self-torture than any game short of Russian roulette. The quicker the average golfer can forget the shot he had dubbed or knocked off-line and concentrate on the next shot . . . the sooner he begins to improve and enjoy golf."

And when we think about it, leadership and life, like a game of golf, can also be humbling. Little good comes from brooding and second guessing and re-living the past mistakes we have made. The next shot . . . in golf or in life, is the big one! In order to lead as we should, one major key is to learn how to put the past behind us and look to the future.

Golf consists of a pleasant walk . . . broken up
by disappointments and bad math.

*I can do everything through Him who
gives me strength* (Phil. 4:13).

This Is a Service Economy

We have been told that we live in a "service" type of economy. But have you noticed how it really works?

First you go to a coin-operated laundry so you can wash and dry your own clothes. Then you drive yourself to a "service" station which is now called a "convenience center" so you can pump your own gas, check your own oil, wash your own windshield, and get your own coffee. The next stop is at one of those banking machines where you make your own deposit and withdraw your own money. Finally, you're off to a fast food restaurant where you go to the counter to place your order, carry your own tray to your table, get your own napkins and plasticware. Then on the way out you are asked to put your trash in a container.

And that's being called a "service" economy!? Where is the service in service? I suspect that if real service were offered customers would beat a path to your place of business.

Have you noticed how delicately balanced our economy is? When the price of cars goes down, gasoline prices go up.

*Though the fig tree does not bud and
there are no grapes on the vines,
though the olive crop fails and the
fields produce no food, though there
are no sheep in the pen and no cattle
in the stalls, yet I will rejoice in the
Lord, I will be joyful in God my Savior*
(Hab. 3:17-18).

The Curse of the Emerald

To the greatest charity event of the season, the lady wore a beautiful, huge, gaudy, emerald pendant. At the hotel ballroom, all the women crowded around her to admire it. She boasted, "This is the third largest emerald in the world. The largest is in the Crown of the Andes, the second belongs to the Queen of England, and then this one, the 'Lefkowitz' emerald."

They were impressed and oooohed and aaaawweed. "How lucky you are, what a jewel," one of the admirers said.

"Wait, nothing in life is that easy," said the dowager. "Unfortunately, the wearer of this emerald must bear the Lefkowitz curse."

The ladies were silent, then one of them asked, "What is the Lefkowitz curse?"

The wearer of the emerald sighed and said, "Abe Lefkowitz!"

For understanding that nothing in life is as easy as it might appear to be.

Then there was the widow in Texas who
remarked that her husband was a total loss . . .
it seems he died without life insurance.

For I am the Lord, your God, who
takes hold of your right hand and says
to you, Do not fear; I will help you
(Isa. 41:13).

Three Dollar's Worth

Here's a bit of provocative prose written by an unknown source, which is like a burr under your saddle of life. . . .

I WOULD LIKE TO BUY THREE DOLLARS WORTH OF GOD PLEASE, I would like just a little. Not enough to explode my soul or disturb my sleep. Not enough to take control of my life . . . I'd like just enough to equal a cup of warm milk, just enough to ease some of the pain of my guilt.

I WOULD LIKE TO BUY THREE DOLLARS WORTH OF GOD . . . I don't want enough of Him to make me love a black man or pick beets with a migrant. I want ecstasy, not transformation. I just want the warmth of the womb, not a new birth. Not enough to impose responsibility. Just enough to make church folks think I'm okay. I want a pound of the Eternal in a paper sack. I would like to buy three dollars worth of God, please!

Some people are really willing and want to
serve God . . . but only as His consultant.

The Lord our God, the Lord is one.
Love the Lord your God with all your
heart and with all your soul and with
all your strength (Deut. 6:4-5).

Do not follow where the path
may lead. Go instead
where there is no path
and leave a trail.

God's Help

Mr. Somekh, age 74, was taking his first trip by air and was assigned a seat next to an Arab wearing a white, flowing robe. The Arab stared at the Jew, buckled in, and spit on Mr. Somekh's shoes.

The plane took off, leveled . . . then the Arab fell asleep and they flew into a storm. Poor Mr. Somekh grabbed for the air-sickness bag and missed . . . all over the Arab's white robe.

The old man fearfully closed his eyes and began to pray, "Help me. When this crazy man awakens and sees his robe, he will kill me with his dagger. Oh, Lord, please, help me!"

In a few minutes, the Arab awakened, stretched. . . . Mr. Somekh, with inspiration, leaned over and politely smiled, "So . . . are you feeling better, now?"

I want to live with divine help in all aspects of leadership and inspiration.

Perhaps the Lord allows some of us to get into trouble because that is the only time we ever think about asking for His help.

God is our refuge and strength, an ever-present help in trouble. Therefore we will not fear, though the earth give way and the mountains fall into the heart of the sea (Ps. 46:1-2).

The Skeptical American

A very skeptical passenger at an airport dropped in a coin and out of the speaker of this inventive device came the following: "You are an American, you are 5'-11" tall, you weigh 174 pounds and you are booked on Flight 369 to San Francisco, California."

The man was incredulous! He was sure it was a practical joke so he ran to the rest room, opened his suitcase and completely changed his clothes, pulled down his hat, hobbled like a shrunken little old man, again dropped in his quarter and waited for the announcement:

"You are still an American, you are 5'-11" tall, you weigh 174 pounds and while you were changing your clothes, your Flight 369 left for San Francisco."

It's sure easy to get sidetracked in our world. There are so many people and so many new things that call for our focus. Decide now to live with priority and focus, not letting anything throw you off your course.

Very few leaders make a deliberate choice
between good and evil . . . the choice is
usually between what we want to do and what
we should do.

*Blessed rather are those who hear the
word of God and obey it* (Luke 11:28).

Target Shooting

A captain of the U.S. Cavalry, following the Civil War, was riding through a small town in Oklahoma, and drew up his horse in astonishment. On the side of a barn he saw about a hundred different chalked bull's-eye circles . . . and in the center of each a round bullet hole! The captain stopped the first man he met. "Who is that marksman? What shooting!"

The passerby slowed, sighed, and said, "That's Tim Decker's boy. He's strange. . . . "

"I don't care what he is," said the Captain, "the cavalry needs anyone who can shoot that well!"

"Ahhh," said the pedestrian, "you don't understand, captain. You see, first little Timmy shoots, then he draws them circles."

Anyone can be a sure-shot if he shoots first and then draws the circle. But a real marksman learns how to center the bull's-eye by diligent, consistent practice!

One real danger for leaders is not that our aim
is too high and we miss it . . . but that our goal
is too low and we hit it.

Set your hearts on things above, where
Christ is seated at the right hand of
God. Set your minds on things above,
not on earthly things (Col. 3:1-2).

Six Commandments for Livin'

Satchel Paige is a name out of baseball's past. He was perhaps the best-known and best-remembered black baseball pitcher who, unfortunately, spent a very short time playing in the major leagues. Not only was he a great pitcher, but "Satchmo" was also known as a philosopher of sorts. Here are his "SIX COMMANDMENTS" on life:

1) Avoid fried food, which angers the blood.

2) When your stomach disrupts you, lay down and pacify it with cool thoughts.

3) Avoid the vices, like carryin' on at night in society, 'cause the social ramble ain't restful.

4) Avoid running at all times.

5) Keep your juices flowin' by janglin' gently as you move.

6) Never look back: something might be gainin' on you.[4]

This world would be a better and a happier place if its leaders had more vision and fewer nightmares.

Seek good, not evil, that you may live. Then the Lord God Almighty will be with you, just as you say He is. Hate evil, love good; maintain justice in the courts (Amos 5:14-15).

Just Ordinary People

Are you ever bothered by the fact that you seem to be so . . . well, just plain ordinary, average, with little or no hope of being a roaring success?

Listen to Joseph D'Arrigo who said, "I've always regarded myself as average. I got into life insurance and did reasonably well. By a fluke, I was put on a committee with several of the biggest sales people in the industry. I was terribly intimidated."

However, he came to realize something important. He goes on, "They were no more geniuses than I was. They were just ordinary people who had set their sights high, then found a way to achieve their goals."

Then, he realized something more, "If other average guys could dream big dreams, so could I!" Today . . . Joe owns his own multi-million-dollar company!

When just plain ordinary people begin to
dream big dreams . . . leaders are born and big
goals are met.

*Jacob "had a dream in which he saw a
stairway resting on the earth, with its
top reaching to heaven, and the angels
of God were ascending and descending
on it"* (Gen. 28:12).

*Leadership: The art of getting
someone else to do something you
want done because he wants to do it.*

Dwight D. Eisenhower (1890 - 1969)

Wreckers

On a moonless, stormy night, some 200 years ago, four men stood on a grassy knoll overlooking the North Atlantic and peered seaward at a ship's light glowing in the darkness. One of the men paced back and forth, leading a horse with a lighted lantern tied to its nodding chin. Soon, now a short distance at sea, the ship, seeing the light of what they assumed to be another ship, sailed in its direction only to go aground and be wrecked. The sand, sea, and wind would eventually hide the wreck but not before everything of value had been taken by these four men and others like them who made their living by treachery.

This describes one of many such instances that took place at Cape Hatteras in North Carolina. More than 2,300 ships met their death here, some by accident and many more by treachery. Leaders keep a sharp eye out for the forces that would destroy and kill.

There seems to be all kinds of leaders . . . but
where are they leading us?

> *He also told them this parable: "Can a*
> *blind man lead a blind man? Will they*
> *not both fall into a pit? A student is not*
> *above his teacher, but everyone who is*
> *fully trained will be like his teacher"*
> (Luke 6:39-40).

Keeping Promises

Do you have a minute to read about one of the major secrets of success? Three women started a West Coast company 14 years ago which furnished model homes for builders. From the first they built their business on simple dependability and not on any strokes of creative genius.

"Because we've never been late with an installation," says Kathy Scroggie, one partner, "we've survived the recession when our competitors were declaring bankruptcy. Once, with a grand opening scheduled for the end of the week and much of our furniture still on a truck somewhere between here and North Carolina, we went out and bought $5,000 worth of items at retail. That ate up most of our profit, but we couldn't let the builder down."

Truth, honesty, dependability, and promise keeping are major corner stones on which to build any life and any business success. It's a discipline that must be developed.

Leaders are noted by at least two
characteristics: first they are people of
integrity; and second, they are able to
influence other people to follow them.

Whatever your lips utter you must be
sure to do, because you made your vow
freely . . . with your own mouth
(Deut. 23:23).

Ivan the Terrible

Ivan "the Terrible" was every bit as bad as his name sounds. This Russian czar tortured thousands of citizens and indulged in long drunken periods. Then, after each wild affair, Ivan would atone by prostrating himself in front of the church altar. He believed he was divinely chosen to rule Russia, so any of his acts, no matter how bad, were acts of God.

He could be eloquent and an able leader but his temper and cruelty were lifelong attributes. He had 60,000 people killed in one city and in a fit of anger struck his 27-year-old son and killed him.

On March 18, 1584, Ivan died. Following the custom of Russian rulers, it was declared he died a monk. His head was shorn and he was buried in monk's robes so as to fool God.

I'm for living life so that none of us have to try to fool God at the moment of our death.

The reason leaders can't lead their followers
in the right direction is because the leaders
aren't going that way themselves.

If you fully obey the Lord your God
and carefully follow all His commands
I give you today, the Lord your God
will set you high above all the nations
on earth. All these blessings will come
upon you and accompany you if you
obey the Lord your God
(Deut. 28:1-2).

Leadership

The definition of leadership is: INFLUENCE!
The key to leadership is: PRIORITIES!
The most important ingredient of leadership is: INTEGRITY!
The ultimate test of leadership is: CREATING
     POSITIVE CHANGE!
The quickest way go gain leadership is: PROBLEM SOLVING!
The extra plus in leadership is: ATTITUDE!
The indispensable quality of leadership is: VISION!
The most appreciable asset in leadership is: DEVELOPING
     PEOPLE!
The price tag of leadership is: SELF-DISCIPLINE!
The most important lesson of leadership is: STAFF
DEVELOPMENT![5]

Modern corporations should be communities, not battlefields. At their heart lie covenants between executives and employees that rest on shared commitment to ideas, to issues, to values, to goals, and to management processes. Words such as love, warmth, and personal chemistry are certainly pertinent. (Max De Pree)

So in everything, do to others what you would have them do to you, for this sums up the Law and the Prophets (Matt. 7:12).

Notes

[1] James C. Georges, ParTraining Corp., from an interview in *Executive Communications,* 1/87.

[2] John Maxwell, *Be a People Person* (Wheaton, IL: Victor Books, 1989).

[3] Mack Sennett, *Book of Blunders* (Kansas City, MO: Hallmark Editions).

[4] Leo Rosten, *Leo Rosten's Giant Book of Laughter* (New York, NY: Bonanza Books).

[5] John C. Maxwell, *Developing the Leader Within You* (Nashville, TN: Thomas Nelson Pub.)

If you enjoyed this book we also have available:

Mini-Moments for Christmas
Mini-Moments for Fathers
Mini-Moments for Graduates
Mini-Moments for Mothers

At bookstores nationwide or write:
New Leaf Press, P.O. Box 726, Green Forest, AR 72638